I0496869

www.strungoutonart.com

STRUNGOUTONART

Powered by:

Strung On Art Out

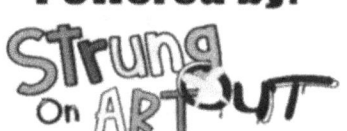

STRUNGOUTONART

STRUNGOUTONART

ILLUSTRATION BY: KENDALL ROGERS

STRUNGOUTONART

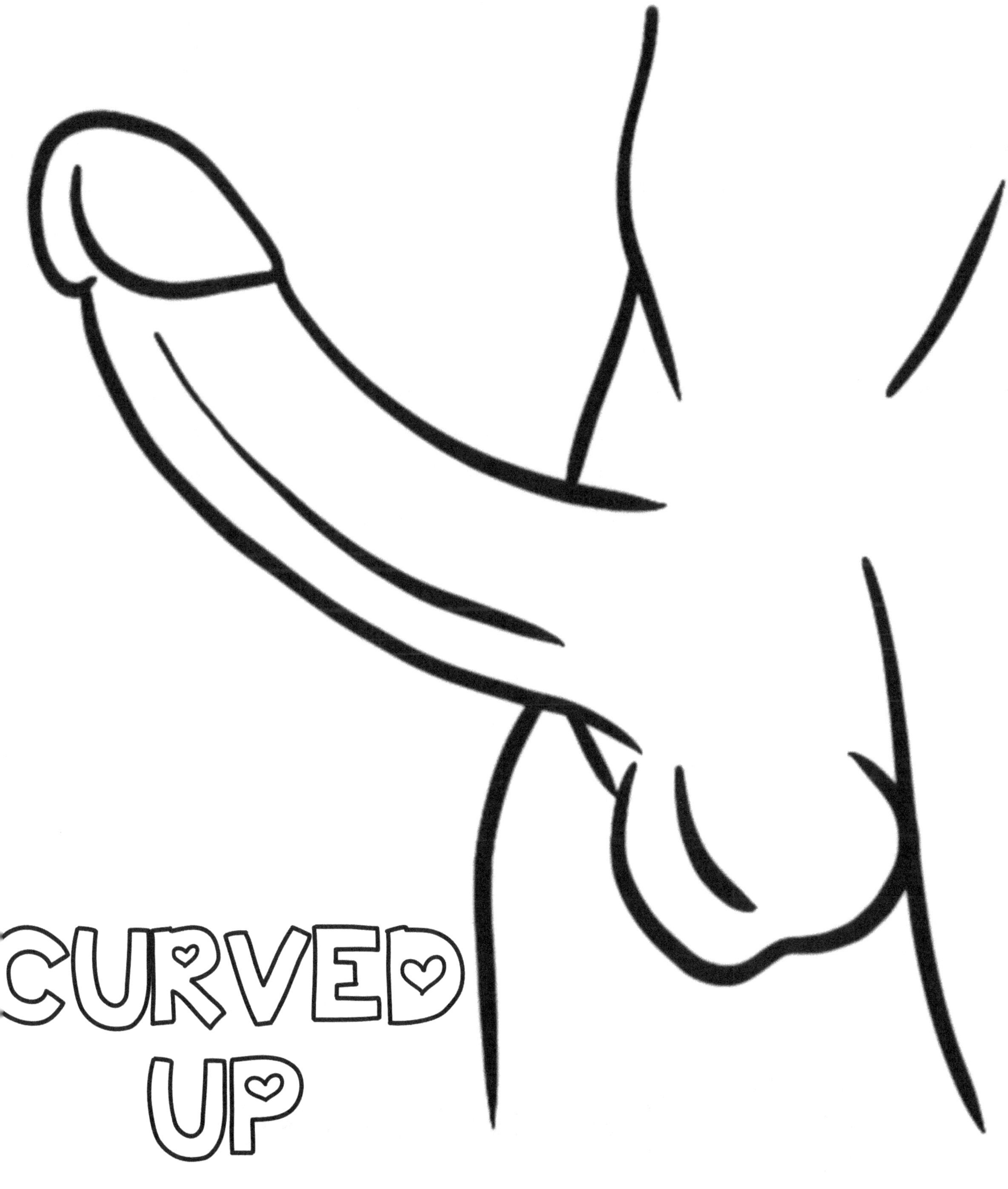
CURVED
UP

STRUNGOUTONART

CURVED DOWN

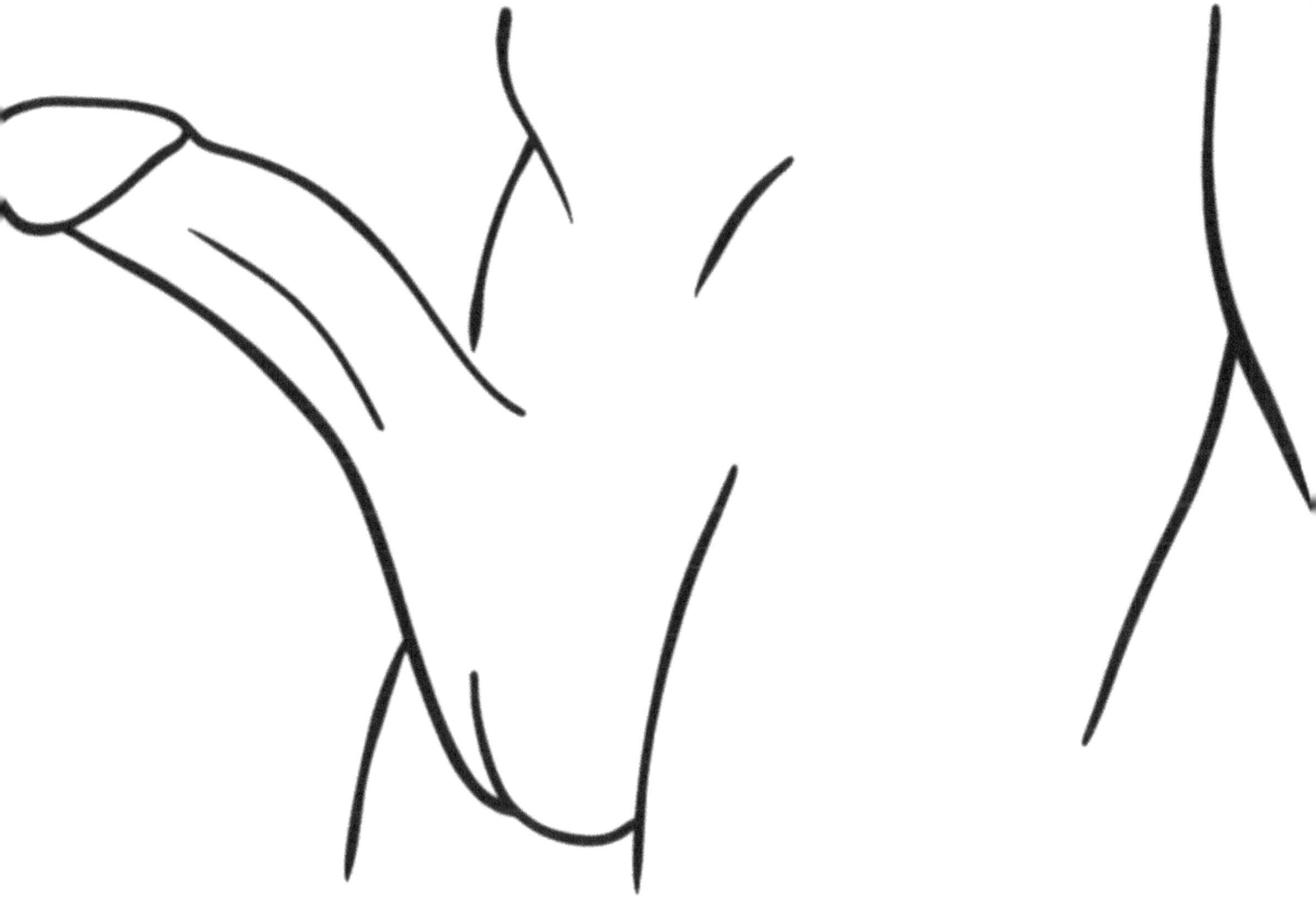

STRUNGOUTONART

C-Shaped

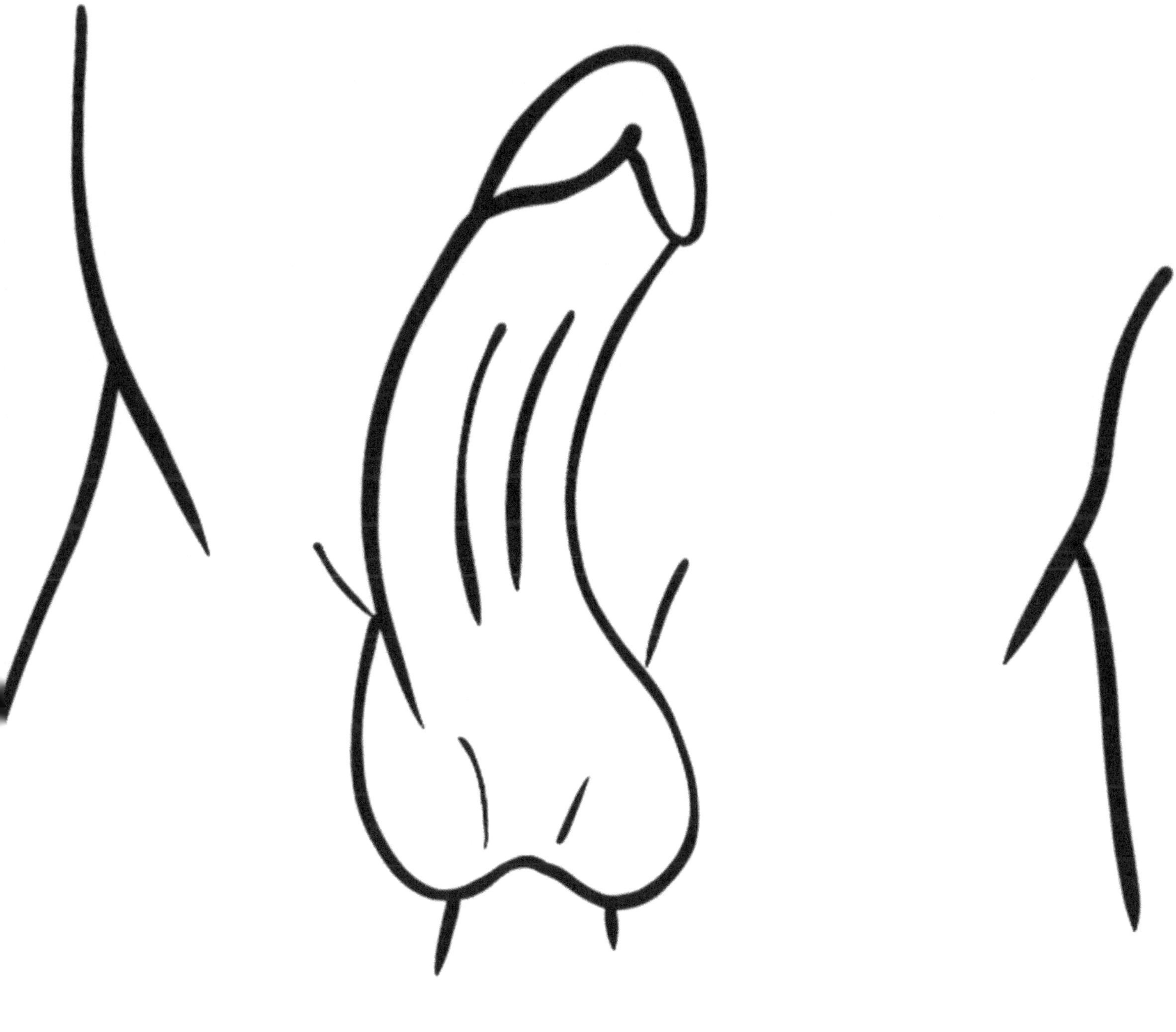

STRUNGOUTONART

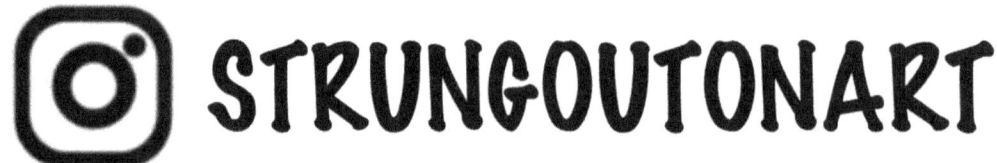

Straight

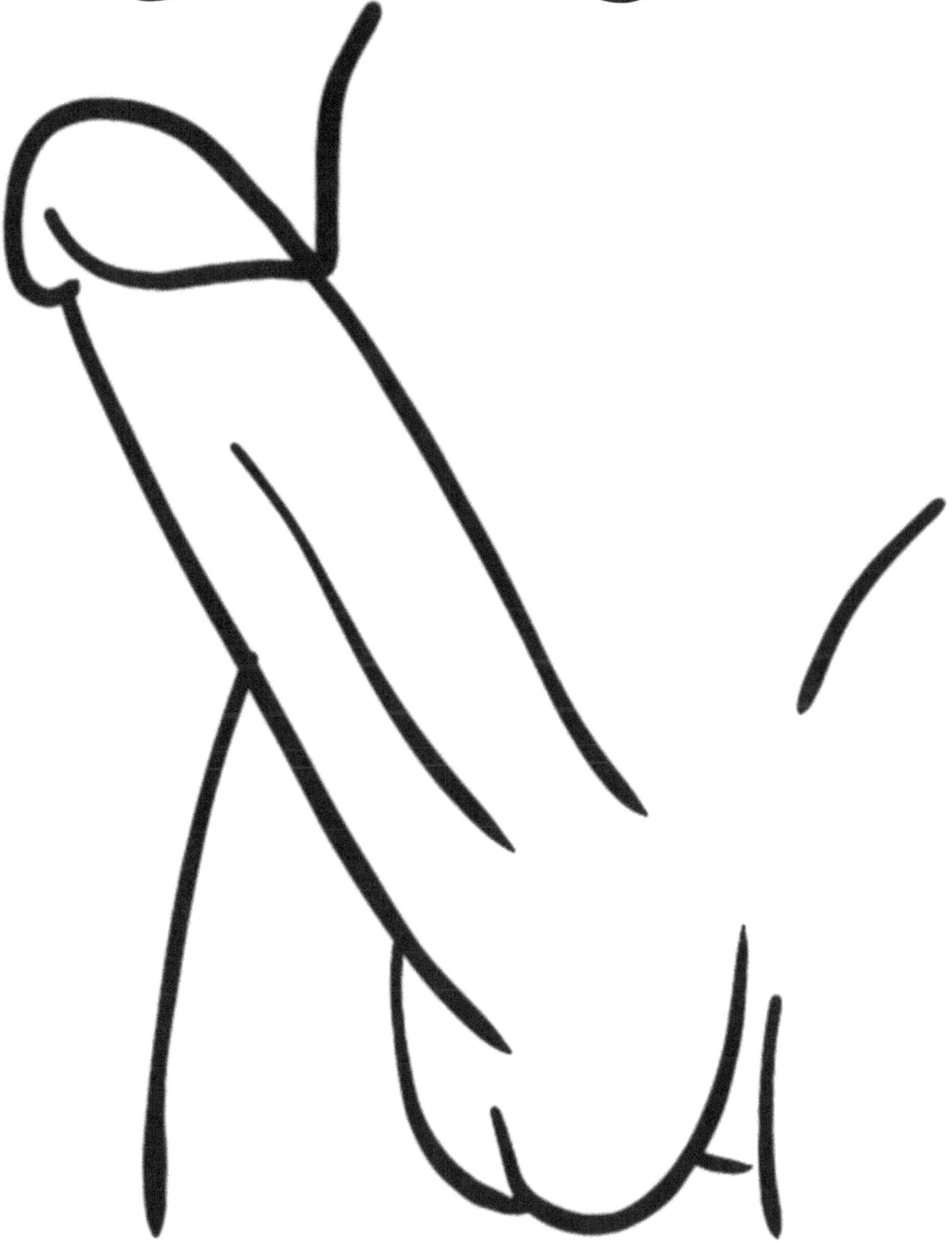

STRUNGOUTONART

Large Based

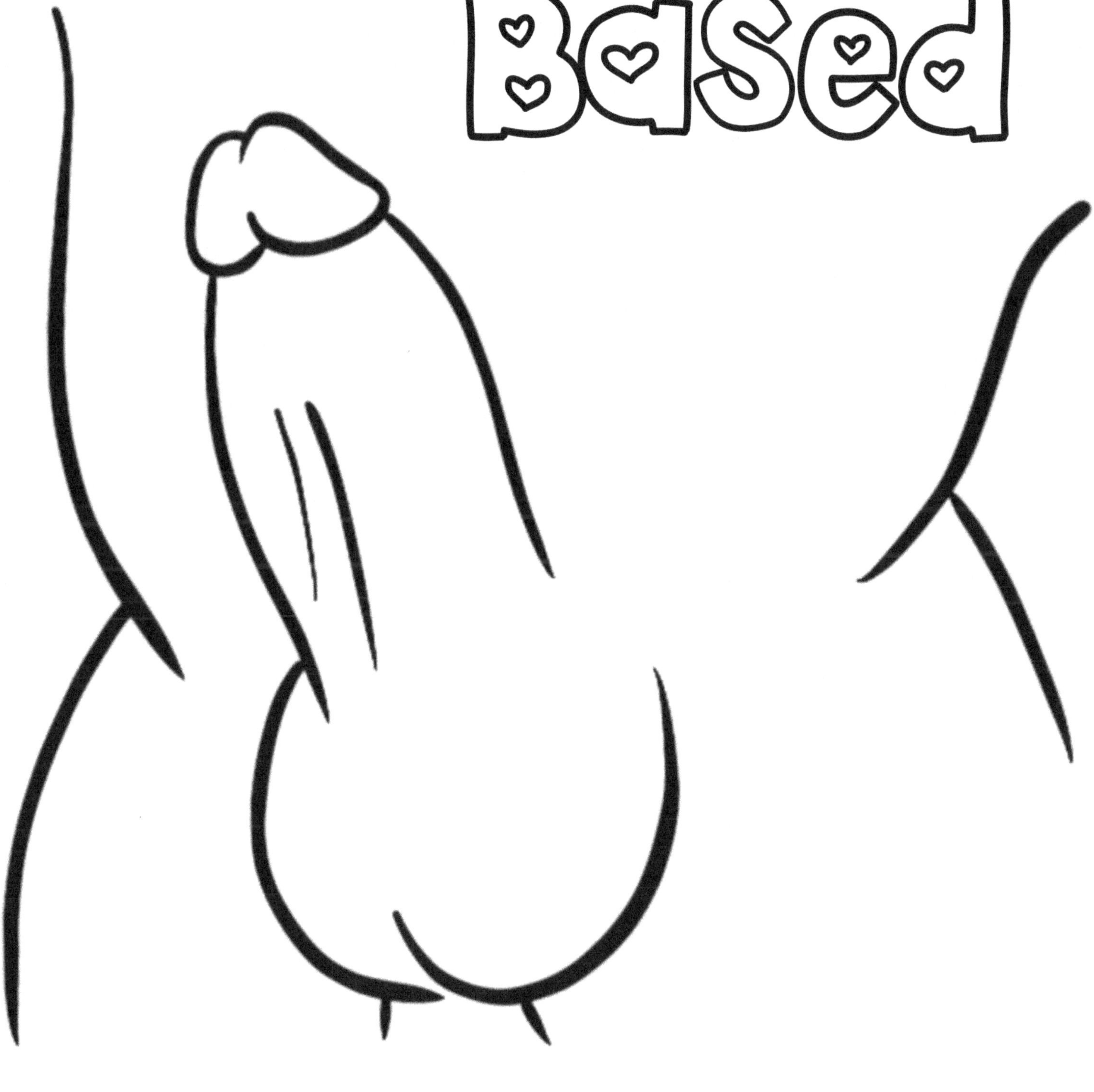

STRUNGOUTONART

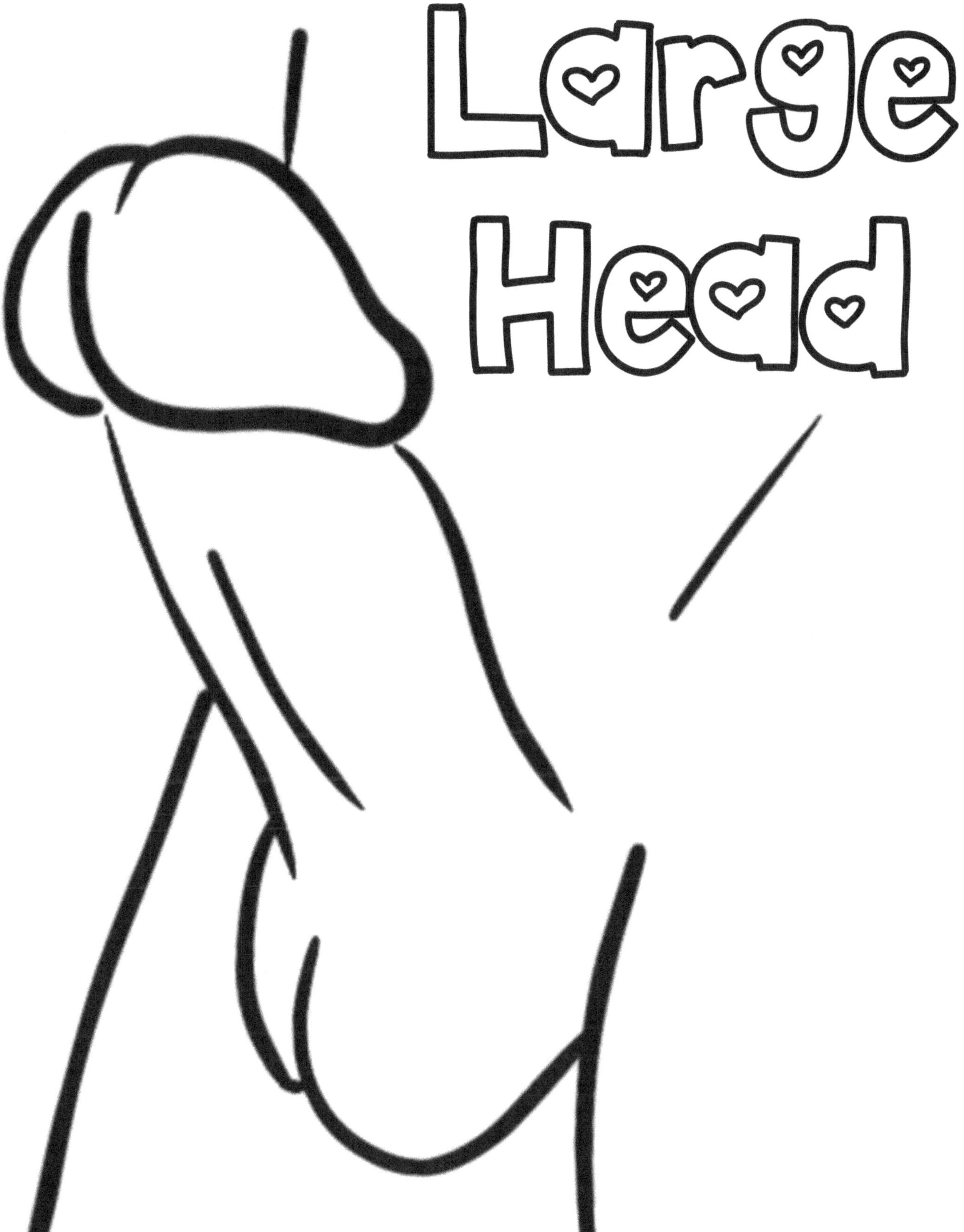
Large Head

STRUNGOUTONART

UNCUT

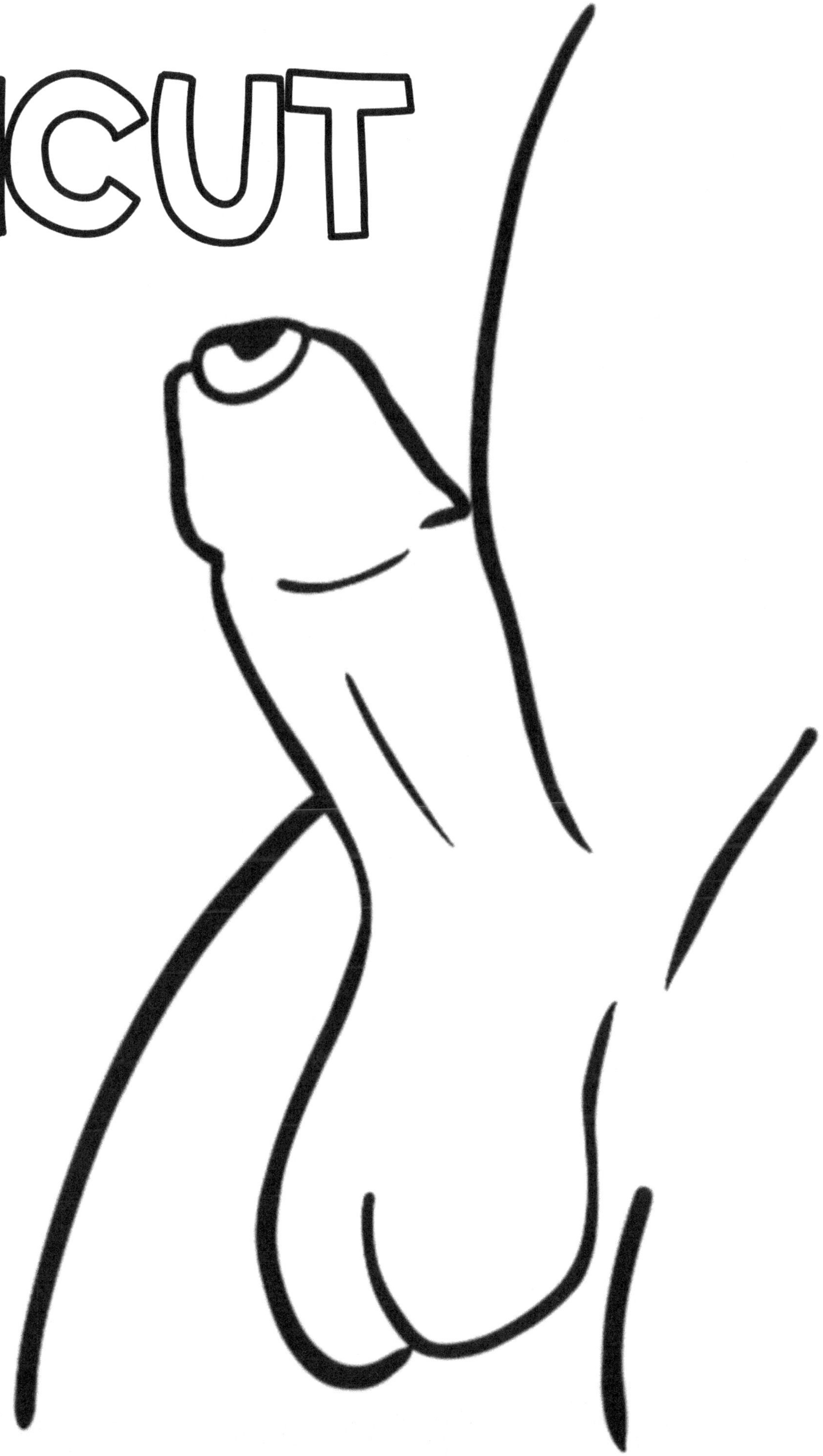

STRUNGOUTONART

Veiny

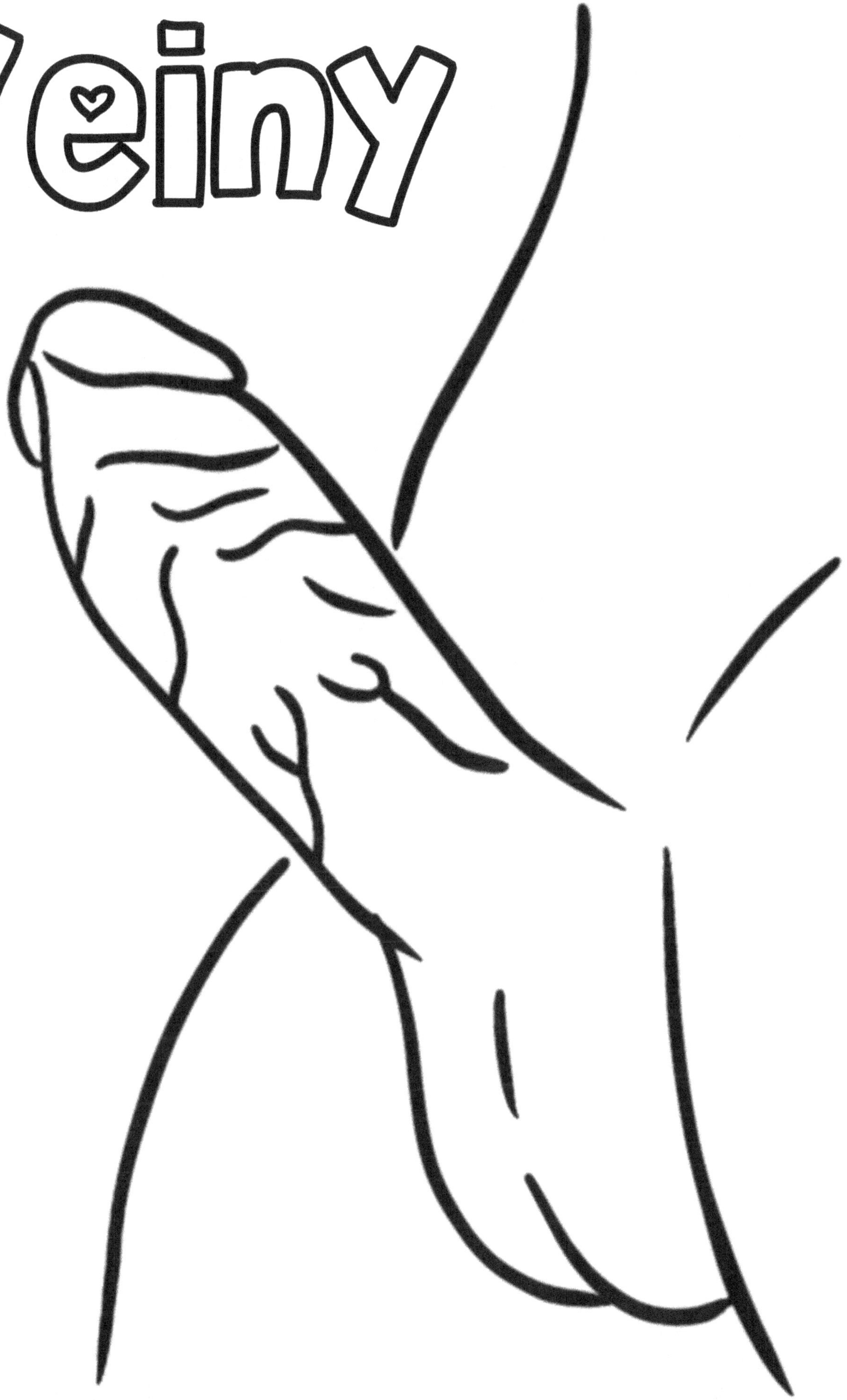

STRUNGOUTONART

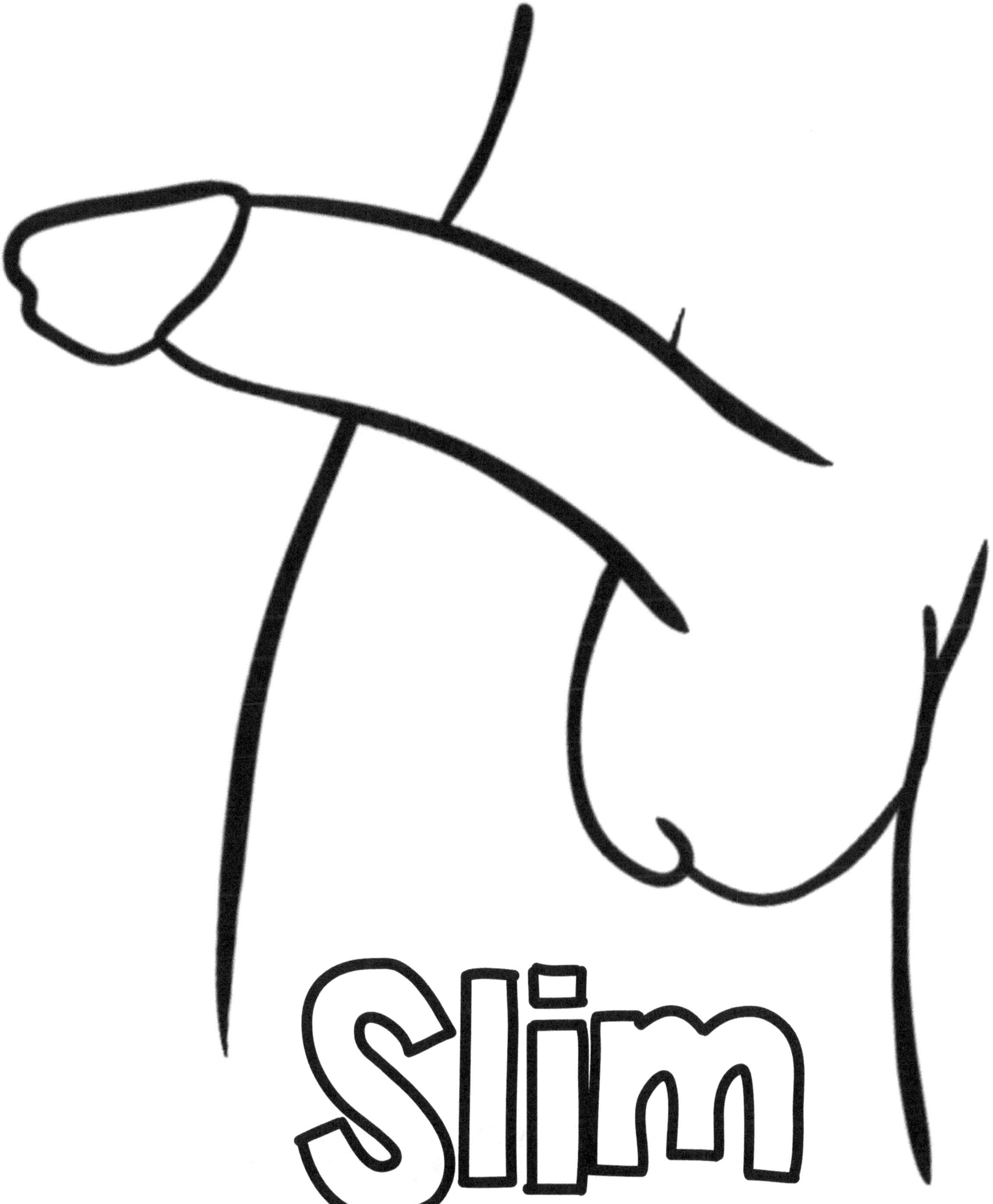
Slim

Thick

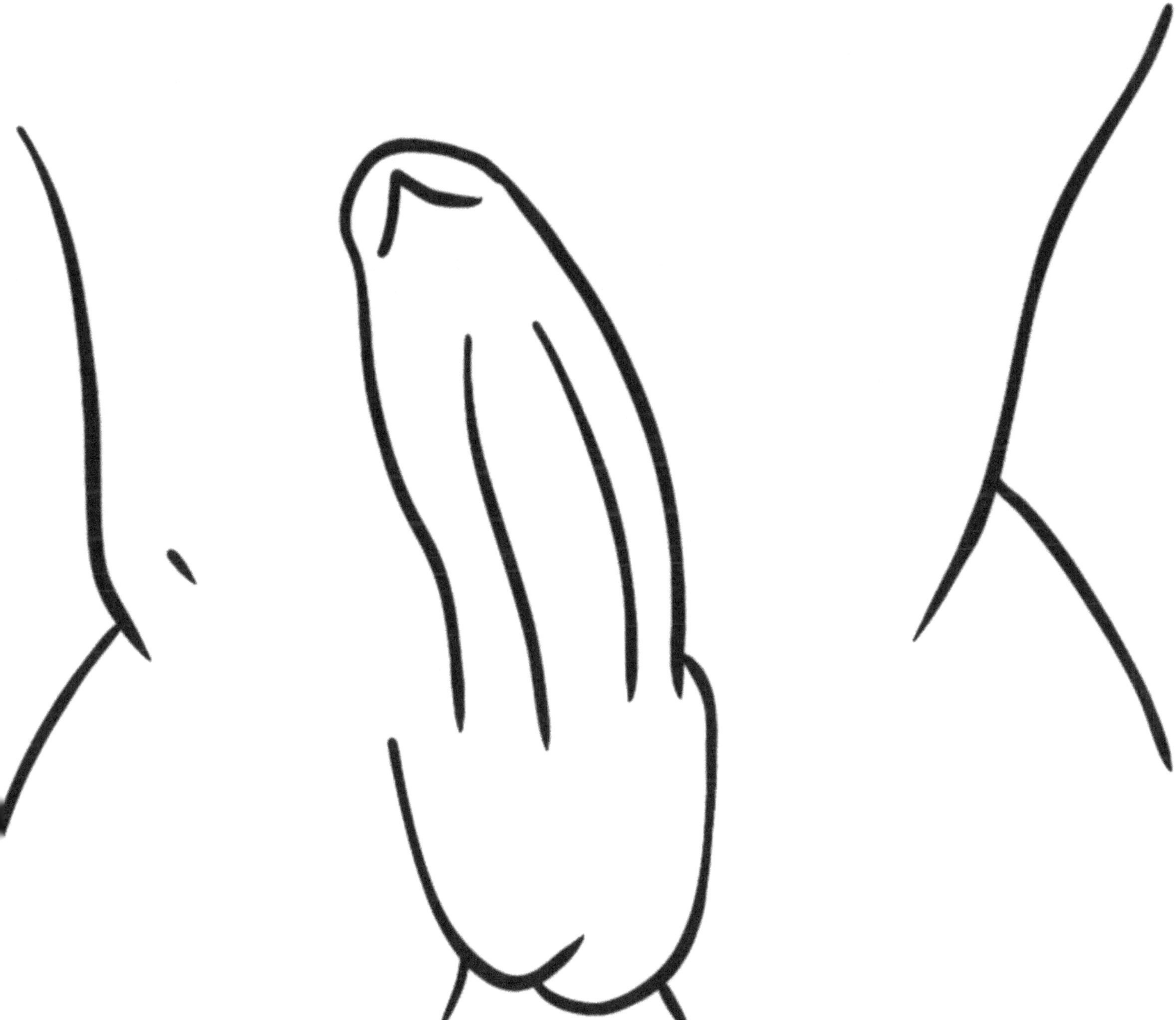

STRUNGOUTONART

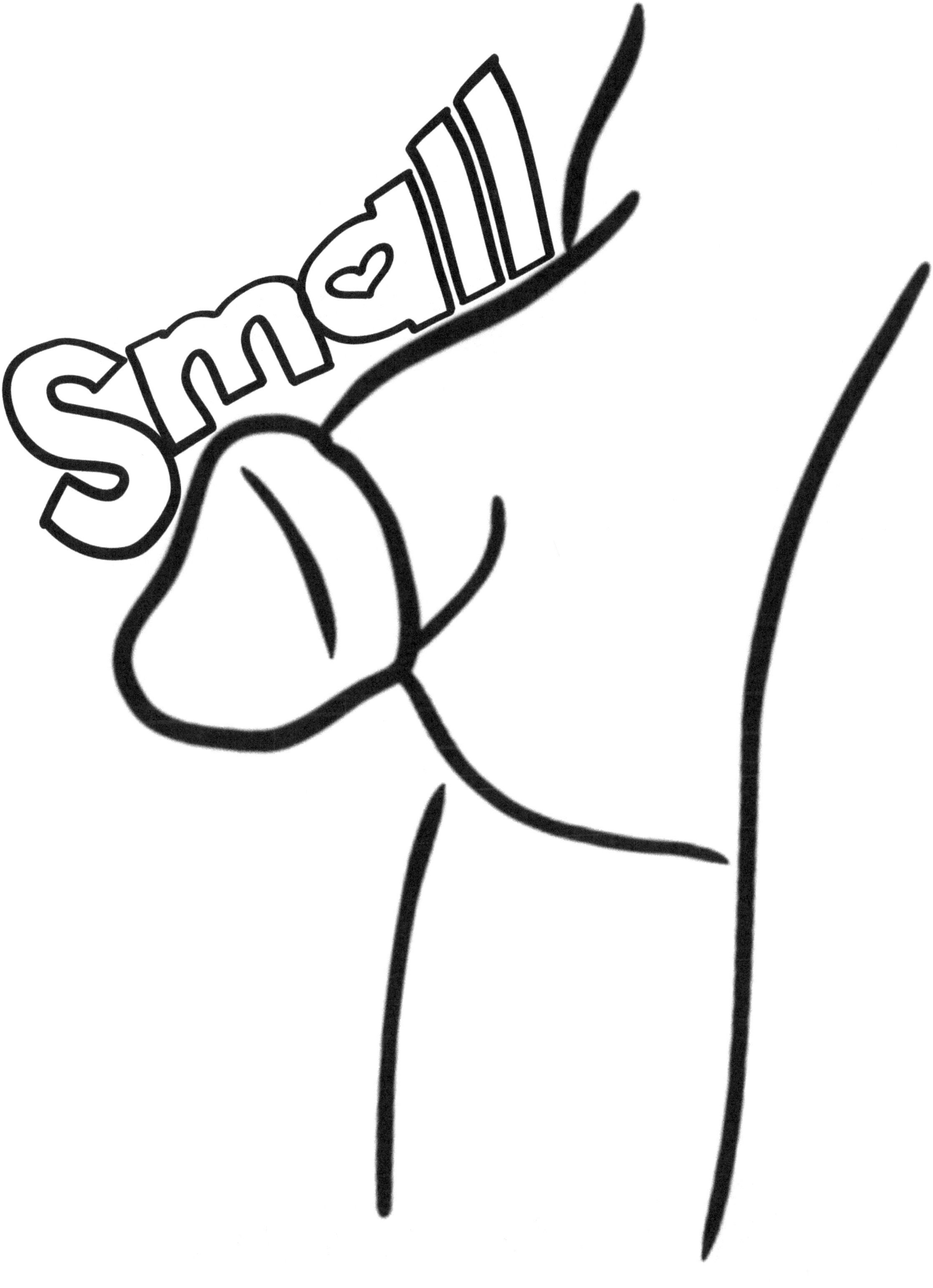
Small

STRUNGOUTONART

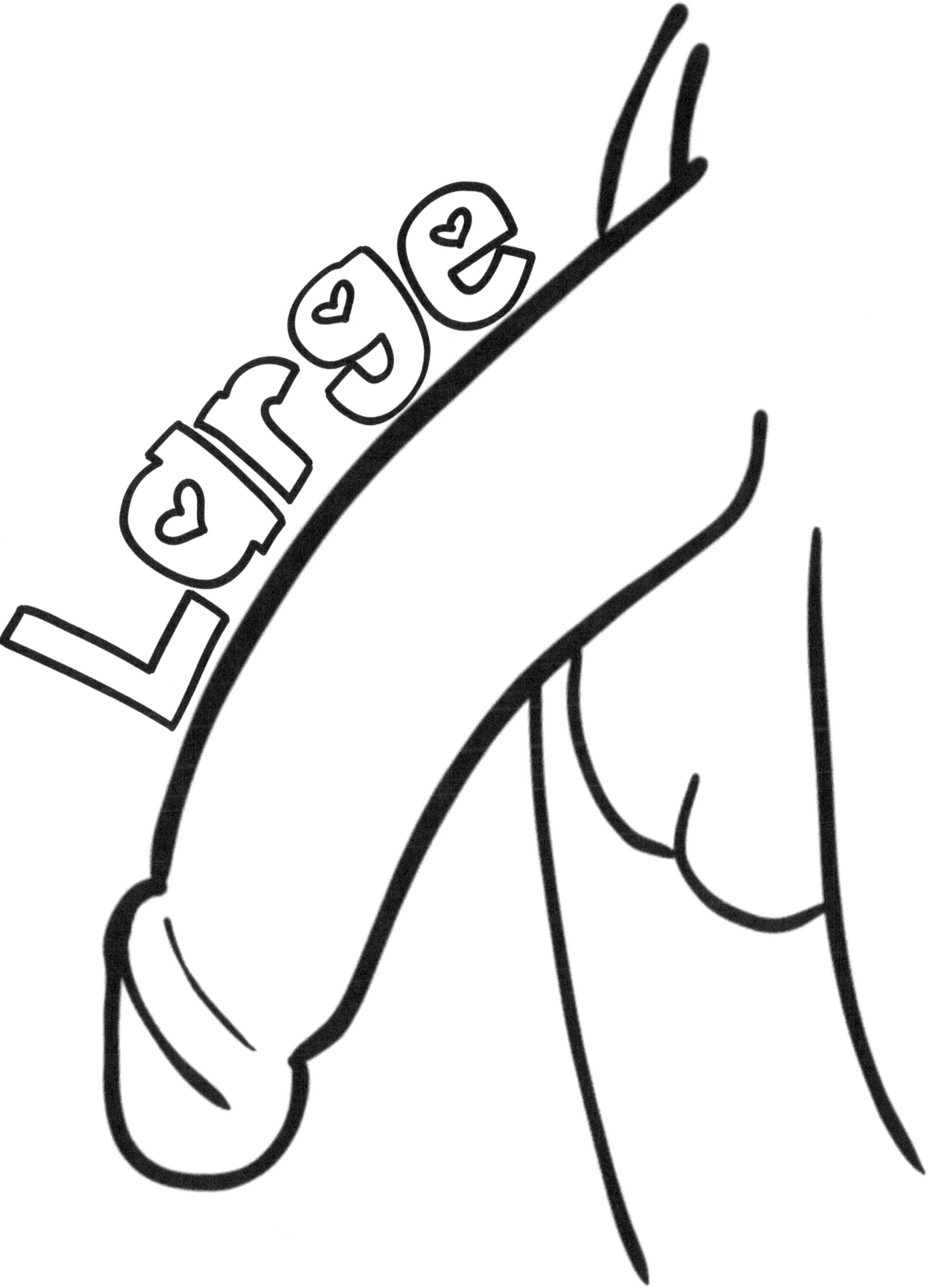
Large

STRUNGOUTONART

www.ingramcontent.com/pod-product-compliance
Lightning Source LLC
Chambersburg PA
CBHW080439220526
45465CB00009B/3357
9798829252601